# In Conversation With...Literary Journals

*Edited by Isabelle Kenyon and Dr Charley Barnes*

First published April 2022 by Fly on the Wall Press

Published in the UK by

Fly on the Wall Press

56 High Lea Rd

New Mills

Derbyshire

SK22 3DP


www.flyonthewallpress.co.uk


ISBN Print: 9781913211752

EBook: 9781913211776

Typesetting and Cover Design by Isabelle Kenyon.

Printed in the UK by Severn, Gloucester on responsibly sourced paper

# Editor's Letter – *by Dr Charley Barnes and Isabelle Kenyon*

It has been a pleasure to read the interviews of these international journals and to see just how much choice is out there for writers, across all genres and styles of writing! Here there are many opportunities for the emerging writer, as well as the more experienced, and we hope this will be a much-thumbed and personal guide for you, throughout your writing journey. Wherever your journal publications take you, I'm sure that you will find the writing community to be a supportive network and a rewarding experience. Thank you to the journal editors who shared their expertise with us this year!

# Contents

*In Conversation with... Nikki Dudley, Managing Director*

*London, UK*

**Pay? N Simultaneous submissions? Y Feedback? Y**

**Online publication? Y**

*We know that your main focus is poetry, but do you ever accept submissions which verge on cross-genre or which are stylistically different to the rest of your publishing aesthetic?*

We love experimental and innovative writing. We love things that cross boundaries and do not fit into a particular genre. This is what we're all about! If you have something weird and new looking for a home, we might just be the place. We also accept intermediary pieces and artwork. We publish all kinds of fiction, poetry and vispo. We also publish work that may appear more traditional but there's something about it which spoke to us, whether it be the tone, the concept or the striking images.

*What is the editorial focus for your literary journal and what have you set out to achieve?*

We want to champion unusual, visually exciting and innovative writing that experiments with expectations. We want to support new and established writers and to consider your work in its own right, without knowing your background. We have strived to make streetcake a welcoming publication, regardless of whether someone is new to the genre or not. We encourage play and exploration. We ask people to send in more than one piece as we like to consider a range of work from a writer, rather than one standalone piece. Most of all though, we want to publish amazing writing and celebrate our writers, especially if they're doing something innovative and playful.

*When are your submission windows?*

We publish every 2 months at present. We generally publish around the 15th.

*How should authors go about approaching you with their writing and is there a best practice?*

Just submit via our email. All the submission guidelines are on the site and we're happy to help you if you drop us an email. Being friendly in your communications is always a big plus for us.

*What are your turnaround times like and do you give unsolicited feedback?*

We say up to 6 weeks' response time for busy periods but we aim to answer sooner than that. We've had a lot of submissions lately so we fill up quickly! We like to give a few lines in any rejection email to help writers find the right home for their work and give them pointers for if they wish to submit again. If we really like a piece, we'll let the writer know they were close to inclusion, as we hope that will encourage them to submit again. Sometimes a particular piece of writing isn't quite working for us but that doesn't mean we're not a fan: if we say we want to see more work, we mean it!

*Do you focus on representing particular voices or geographical locations?*

No, we are international and open to all voices. We strongly encourage everyone to submit, publishing record or not. It's true that we tend to prefer more non-traditional pieces but a quick read of our previous issues and website should help writers decide if we'll enjoy their work.

*Would you expect to see a cover letter from a writer and if so, what would you love to see in it?*

We only ask for a brief 3rd person bio (which we read after the submission) and a friendly hello is always welcome. We don't need loads of spiel or qualifications but writers can provide a short intro to the piece you're submitting if you feel it's necessary. We have sometimes asked writers to clarify the context of a piece when reading, which has really helped us absorb the piece of writing better.

**Contact Details:**

streetcakemagazine@gmail.com / www.streetcakemagazine.com

# STREET CAKE

## experimental writing magazine

@ since 2008

we enjoy a range of innovat
forms, including visual poet
unconventional ideas a
presentations, hybrid form
asemic writing, uniq
imagery, playing with form
and perspectives, non line
writing, intermedia piec
collages, and much mo

# poetry, fiction and visp

bimonthly online publication
experimental writing prize 2019, 2020 and 2021 funded by ACE

*In Conversation with... James Penha, Editor*

*Bali, Indonesia*

**Pay? N Simultaneous submissions? N Feedback? N**

**Online publication? Y**

*What is the editorial focus for your literary journal and what have you set out to achieve?*

Since 2005, The New Verse News has sought and published, on a daily basis, progressive, timely poems on the news of the day in order to allow writers to share their immediate artistic responses to current events. Our submission window is always open. We have been known to publish work on the same day it is submitted! Thus, we cannot accept simultaneous submissions but promise to respond quickly; certainly in no longer than a fortnight.

*How should authors go about approaching you with their writing and is there a best practice?*

The poem(s) and a brief bio pasted in an e-mail to nvneditor@gmail.com.

*Do you focus on representing particular voices or geographical locations?*

We focus on excellent poetry with points of view which enhance the news rather than just repeating it, but we are proud to represent the widest possible array of voices and locations.

**Contact Details:**

The New Verse News

nvneditor@gmail.com

*In Conversation with... Deborah Edgeley, Editor*

*Cheshire, UK*

**Pay? N Simultaneous submissions? N Feedback? N Online publication? Y**

*What is the editorial focus for your literary journal and what have you set out to achieve?*

The editorial focus for Ink Pantry is to provide a platform to encourage and support writers who are new to the literary world, by publishing their work, as well as to promote the work of more experienced writers, bringing them together as a creative community. Our Ink Pantry volunteers are all writers themselves.

*When are your submission windows?*

We accept submissions on a continual basis, and often have seasonal competitions.

*How should authors go about approaching you with their writing and is there a best practice?*

To provide any social media links, a short author bio (max 100 words), an author jpg (optional), and to paste work in the body of the email, for formatting reasons (no PDFs). We also do special features and author interviews when requested.

**Contact Details:**

Deborah Edgeley, Ink Pantry Publishing

Email: deborah@inkpantry.com

*In Conversation with… Mark Antony Owen, Poet and Publisher*

*Hampshire, UK*

**Pay? N Simultaneous submissions? N Feedback? N
Online publication? Y**

*What is the editorial focus for your literary journal and what have you set out to achieve?*

The idea is to showcase emerging talent alongside established poets, with the emphasis heavily weighted towards lesser-known poets. To bring these voices to life more vividly, each poet gets to share not only their words but also recordings of themselves reading their own work.

*When are your submission windows?*

The aim is to achieve an 18-month submissions cadence. This would mean 'auditions' (the journal is text based but supported by audio – each poet has to include recorded readings of their poems) would open for just one week every year and a half. This may not sound all that generous, but the journal's popularity means it's massively oversubscribed. A week of auditions/submissions can result in enough acceptances to fill a two-year publishing schedule!

*Do you focus on representing particular voices or geographical locations?*

All poets from everywhere in the world can audition so long as the greater part of the poems they submit are written and read in English. In terms of representation, there is a tendency towards prioritising poets who are female, or who identify as such.

**Contact Details:**

iambapoet.com / iamb.online.poetry@gmail.com

*In Conversation with... Ana Savković, Editor in Chief*

*Zagreb, Croatia*

**Pay? N Simultaneous submissions? Y Feedback? N
Online publication? Y**

*What is the editorial focus for your literary journal and what have you set out to achieve?*

ZiN Daily recognizes literature and art as testaments of anguish and catalysts for progress. We are searching for work that will instigate societal and individual change.

*When are your submission windows?*

ZiN Daily is open for submissions year-round.

*What are your turnaround times like and do you give unsolicited feedback?*

Authors may expect a response within 60 days. We don't give unsolicited feedback.

**Contact Details:**

Submissions: zindaily.subs1@gmail.com.

Guidelines: https://zvonainari.hr/zin-daily.

*In Conversation with... Alan Parry, Co-Founding Editor*

*Southport, UK*

**Pay? N Simultaneous submissions? N Feedback? Y**
**Online publication? Y Print publication? Y**

*What is the editorial focus for your literary journal and what have you set out to achieve?*

We aim to create a reputable, democratic literary press. More than this, we wish to lift young and emerging writers by placing them alongside established artists. We run live online events, and events in person when permitted. We have a strong sense of place, in the north of England, and want to share local and regional voices with the world.

*When are your submission windows?*

We have two regular submission windows for The Broken Spine Artist Collective; they are April and October. We open for Flash Fiction periodically, and other potential publication opportunities are made visible across our socials. Contributors receive free copies.

*How should authors go about approaching you with their writing and is there a best practice?*

Authors should read and follow our submission guidelines closely. If you pay attention your submission will not be wasted and has a greater chance of acceptance. We do not request long cover letters, just that writers have paid attention, are patient in waiting for a response, and are polite. We like it when writers are open to editorial suggestions: if we offer them, we see value in your work.

**Contact Details:**

The Broken Spine, thebrokenspine.co.uk

mail@thebrokenspine.co.uk

Twitter: @BrokenSpineArts

**Pay? Y Simultaneous submissions? Y Feedback? Y
Online publication? Y Print publication? Y**

*We know that your main focus is flash fiction, but do you ever accept submissions which verge on cross-genre or which are stylistically different to the rest of your publishing aesthetic?*

Yes! We love to feature hybrid pieces, including comics, text-based artwork and pieces which make use of graphical elements. We recently published a short story told through a collection of receipts, for example. We're always interested in pushing boundaries and exploring new forms, and encourage writers to try us with their strangest and most interesting work.

*What are your turnaround times like and do you give unsolicited feedback?*

We try to respond as quickly as possible, but we do get a lot of submissions and reading through them can take time. For anyone who supports the magazine in any way we make an effort to expedite submissions, and respond with a few helpful notes.

*Would you expect to see a cover letter from a writer and if so, what would you love to see in it?*

A cover letter is very helpful. It's a great place to let us know about things like previous publications, special formatting requirements, or how you found out about Neon. The advice we always give about cover letters is to keep them simple - they don't need to grab anyone's attention or sell the piece you're submitting. Really, they're just a way of saying hello and conveying any relevant information.

**Contact Details:**

www.neonbooks.org.uk

info@neonbooks.org.uk

*In Conversation with… Michael J. DeLuca, Publisher*

*Lake Orion, USA*

**Pay? Y Simultaneous submissions? Y Feedback? Y
Online publication? Y Print publication? Y**

*What is the editorial focus for your literary journal and what have you set out to achieve?*

We publish creative writing in all the forms that fit on the theme of environmental justice. The idea is to give readers a sense of the breadth (and diversity) of impact the extractive capitalist colonial economic model has on humans everywhere, while also inspiring our readers through the passion of our writers: people are working and thinking together, to resist.

*When are your submission windows?*

Reckoning is always open to submissions. We want to give marginalized writers everywhere every opportunity we can to contribute.

*What are your turnaround times like and do you give unsolicited feedback?*

Response times vary but are in the area of three months. We don't provide feedback on every submission, but we try to give submitters at least a brief sense of why a particular piece didn't work for us.

**Contact Details:**

https://reckoning.press

Twitter @ReckoningMag

## In Conversation with... Sam Smith, Editor

### Bridgend, UK

**Pay? N Simultaneous submissions? N Feedback? N Online publication? N Print publication? Y**

*What is the editorial focus for your literary journal and what have you set out to achieve?*

The Journal began circa 1995 as The Journal of Contemporary Anglo-Scandinavian Poetry, but by issue ten had run out of Scandinavian translations. Since then, although most poems we publish are from the UK, I usually manage to find some international work, lately translations from the Spanish by Laura Chalar. The submission guidelines say that I like poems that can cross borders, that don't require shared knowledge. What it doesn't say is that I also like poems that take chances— in either content, format or style. I have also built up a team of prize-winning reviewers.

My aim has always been to encourage honest participation in poetry. Good, original writing is all that I ask for, in whatever format it arrives. But honesty is the most important, which is why I attempt to get every publication sent to us reviewed. I am very proud of The Journal's excellent team of reviewers.

*When are your submission windows?*

Submissions are all year round, whether by post or email. I usually try to respond within a month.

*How should authors go about approaching you with their writing and is there a best practice?*

Submit either by post or email. If by post, an SAE is required. If by email and with an attachment, then make it a Word Doc file, not a PDF. The Journal doesn't carry biographies, only where contributors are currently based, so don't bother with a lengthy biog. Just a polite how-de-do. We post a contributor's complimentary copy within the UK.

**Contact Details:**

Sam Smith, The Journal

38 Pwllcarn Terrace, Blaengarw, Bridgend, CF32 8AS

asamsmith@hotmail.com

https://samsmithbooks.weebly.com/the-journal.html

*In Conversation with... Michelle Tudor, Editor*

*Shropshire, UK*

**Pay? N Simultaneous submissions? Y Feedback? N
Online publication? Y**

*When are your submission windows?*

We work on a rolling submissions basis and all work will be considered for the next open issue.

*How should authors go about approaching you with their writing and is there a best practice?*

We would always suggest reading the guidelines before submitting, but more so, reading some of our previous issues to get an idea of the types of work we are looking for.

*Do you focus on representing particular voices or geographical locations?*

Though we are UK-based, we have never limited our publication geographically. We always strive to present a diverse selection of voices and experiences, and we are particularly interested in publishing marginalised authors and their works.

**Contact Details:**

readwildness.com

twitter.com/platypuspress

instagram.com/platypuspress

platypuspress.co.uk

*In Conversation with... Doug Mathewson, Editor*

*CT. USA*

**Pay? N Simultaneous submissions? Y Feedback? N Print publication? Y**

*We know that your main focus is flash fiction, but do you ever accept submissions which verge on cross-genre or which are stylistically different to the rest of your publishing aesthetic?*

Blink-Ink publishes fiction of approximately 50 words in length. We read and respond to all submissions and inquiries.

Our issues are themed, so please check our website and Facebook. We publish contemporary short fiction, and strive to make it accessible to the reader.

We always welcome art submissions for our covers, but please keep in our format in mind, (5 1/2 X 4 1/4 inches and 20 or so pages). Artwork should relate, even if loosely, to the issue's theme. www.blink-ink.org

*What is the editorial focus for your literary journal and what have you set out to achieve?*

Our focus is to be inclusive rather than exclusive regarding both contributors and readers. We seek a diverse group of writers and readers. We want our journal to be accessible and open to all, as we publish the finest contemporary short fiction. We publish in print, on a quarterly basis. Currently we are in our 13th year of publication.

*When are your submission windows?*

We are a quarterly print journal. New issues come out the first of March, June, September, and December. Submissions for the next issue open the same day, and remain open for approximately forty five days (till the 15th of the following month). We try to notify writers within a week or two about their submissions. If you have not heard back from us after 30 days, please let us know and we will follow up. No attachments, bios, or poetry please. Send submissions in the body of an email to blinkinkinfo@gmail.com. Enquiries also welcome.

**Contact Details:**

More info can be found at www.blink-ink.org

Blink-Ink / blinkinkinfo@gmail.com

*In Conversation with… Lisa Schantl, Founder and Editor-in-Chief*
*Graz, Austria*

## Pay? N Simultaneous submissions? Y Feedback? Y
## Online publication? Y

*We know that your focus is on genres poetry, short fiction and non-fiction, but do you ever accept submissions which verge on cross-genre or which are stylistically different to the rest of your publishing aesthetic?*

Yes. Although our online journal's website shows the categories fiction (short stories and flash fiction), nonfiction (personal essays and creative flash nonfiction) and poetry, we definitely have one or two pieces in each issue that cannot be clearly ascribed to either or. We then engage in a discussion with the author and publish their work under the label they see best. The line between poetry and creative nonfiction can be particularly thin and an interesting border area to dwell in. We want to show appreciation for the creativity and experimentality of our writers, and provide space for their artistic freedom.

*What is the editorial focus for your literary journal and what have you set out to achieve?*

Tint Journal focuses on non-native English writing. In our biannual issues, we publish stories and poems by writers who choose to express their literary voice in the world's most spoken second language, English, which is also not their mother tongue. Our mission is to encourage these writers to stand behind their non-native English backgrounds. Their language has a uniquely modifying quality that enriches their stories and, consequently, their readers' responses to their stories. Through their innovative, tinted lenses, we shine a light on the ways that authors all over the globe contribute to what we know as literature in English.

*When are your submission windows?*

Our issues are not themed and open to all subject matters. For our spring issues, writers and artists are asked to submit their work from mid-October to the end of November in the preceding year, and for our fall issues from mid-April to the end of May.

*How should authors go about approaching you with their writing and is there a best practice?*

As our focus is on non-native English writers, we have to make sure that the writers who we decide to publish belong to this group. To do so, we have a title page request in our submission guidelines which asks the writers to provide their name, first language/mother tongue(s), second or foreign language(s), and nationality on the first page of their document. We cannot consider submissions which do not meet this request. Also, the naming of their submitted file is important as we cannot afford Submittable and sort our submissions by hand: [Category]_[Last Name]_[Title].

*What are your turnaround times like and do you give unsolicited feedback?*

We ask the writers to allow for a period of 20 to 30 days between the end of an open call and our answer. As soon as a call has ended, poetry editor, John, and prose editor, Matt, as well as I, assemble the next issue with great care. The accepted texts undergo developmental and copy editing conducted by our skilled volunteer editors.

Writers whose work does not get accepted can request feedback which we will provide before the start of the next open call, for a small donation to the journal. We do not provide unsolicited feedback.

*Do you focus on representing particular voices or geographical locations?*

Yes, Tint Journal is, as far as our research goes, the world's first and only journal with an exclusive focus on non-native English writing. This means that the writers we publish write in English as their second or foreign language. We seek to represent a wide variety of these voices, emerging and established writers who deal with diverse and probably also under-represented subject matters, texts from various cultures and geographical regions which show strong identities and powerful language use. So far, we have been able to publish writers identifying with 54 different nationalities within six issues.

*Would you expect to see a cover letter from a writer and if so, what would you love to see in it?*

No, we do not read elaborate cover letters. For us, the title page request is all that matters in the first stage. If a text is accepted, we then ask the writer to provide us with a short biographical statement and ask them to answer four questions which we publish as a brief Q&A with every writer to give them more space for expressing the creative voice in our journal. Also, we ask every writer to audio record their text to add an additional layer to the reception of the non-native English texts.

**Contact Details:**

Tint Journal, Lisa Schantl (Founder and Editor-in-Chief), info@tintjournal. com, www.tintjournal.com

*In Conversation with... Linda Black, Editor*
*London, UK*

**Pay? N Simultaneous submissions? N Feedback? N**
**Online publication? Y Print Publication? Y**

*We know that your main focus is poetry but do you ever accept submissions which verge on cross-genre or which are stylistically different to the rest of your publishing aesthetic?*

We are the only UK poetry journal focusing entirely on long poems and sequences. Keen to promote diversity of form and content, we are interested in both traditional and innovative forms, and represent a diverse range of poets and poetic styles from around the world. We have published translations from more than ten languages. Each issue has an essay on an aspect of the long poem. Reviews of books consisting mainly of long poems are published online. We welcome suggestions for essays and reviews. In our online feature, Poets & their Processes, we invite poets to write about their writing!

*What is the editorial focus for your literary journal and what have you set out to achieve?*

Since our inception we have striven to publish an equal number of women and men, and to foster a sense of community and engagement across styles, languages, cultures and countries. We like to bring people together and hope to return to our wonderful launches, held in the Barbican Library. Our editorials are wide-reaching; we aim to reflect the range of poems, of poets, context, subject matter within each issue, our appreciation of both poets and our audience, plus wider contexts such as the writing life. Every poem we publish has a 250-word introduction focusing not on the bio of our poets but on their writing processes.

*When are your submission windows?*

Our submission windows are the months of June and November.

Submissions guidelines:

1. Poems sent outside this time will not be kept.

2. We do not accept simultaneous submissions.

3. We do not publish the same poet/s in consecutive issues.

4. Two poems maximum per issue.

5. Each poem must be at least 75 lines long (no book length poems).

6. Poems must be unpublished.

7. Put your name and poem title on each page. Save in your own name + title, e.g. 'Joe Bloggs Happy Days.doc' , NOT longpoem.doc or submission.doc

8. Send to longpoemmagazine@gmail.com in Word.doc or docx files.

9. We do not accept paper submissions or submissions sent in the body of an email.

**Contact Details**

Editor: Linda Black

Deputy Editor, Claire Crowther

www.longpoemmagazine.org.uk

mail@longpoemmagazine.org.uk

## In Conversation with... J.L. Corbett, Editor
### UK

**Pay? N Simultaneous submissions? Y Feedback? N
Online publication? Y**

*What is the editorial focus for your literary journal and what have you set out to achieve?*

Idle Ink is a publisher of curious fiction. This can be interpreted in many different ways, and we delight in all of them.

I created Idle Ink because I couldn't get my work published anywhere and I was tired of waiting for other magazines to take a chance on my off-kilter stories. Idle Ink has become a sanctuary for weird fiction, the whimsical, murky sort of fiction that doesn't fit anywhere else. We give every sort of story a chance; the stranger, the better.

*What are your turnaround times like and do you give unsolicited feedback?*

I aim to get back to submitters within a month. I no longer provide unsolicited feedback— not everybody wants it and due to the average volume of submissions, it's just not feasible. I always get back to submitters whether it's a 'no' or a 'yes', and so I encourage writers to send a follow up email if they've not heard anything back within that time frame. It probably means that their email has slipped through the cracks (though to my knowledge, this has only ever happened once or twice).

*Would you expect to see a cover letter from a writer and if so, what would you love to see in it?*

Honestly? Cover letters aren't that important. It's polite to send one, but it won't impact my decision.

Every so often, I'll get a blank email with a story attached— no name, no hello, nothing. That's a little jarring. I also get submissions from the other end of the spectrum— ones with less of a cover letter, more of a personal essay (which is really unnecessary). All you need to write to be in my good books is a quick introduction, *'Hi, my name is X, I'd like to submit my storY 'X' (x words), hope you enjoy it!'*. Bam! Done.

**Contact Details:**

Twitter & Instagram: @_IdleInk_

Email: idleink@outlook.com

*In Conversation with… Charlotte Cosgrove, Editor*
Liverpool, UK

**Pay? N Simultaneous submissions? Y Feedback? N
Online publication? Y**

*We know that your main focus is poetry, but do you ever accept submissions which verge on cross-genre or which are stylistically different to the rest of your publishing aesthetic?*

As a poetry journal we aim to be as expansive as possible. Any form of poetry is welcome whether that's in a traditional form, experimental or even prose poems. The poems we choose are often divergent in order to broaden people's interest and experience of poetry as a whole. It's often so easy to think you don't like poetry because you've only ever come across one 'type'. We've also begun a new flash feature on our website with an aim to showcase the talents of a fiction writer each submission round.

*What is the editorial focus for your literary journal and what have you set out to achieve?*

Rough Diamond came into being with an extremely open mind! We wanted as many different types of poems as possible. One of my main aims was to make sure writers felt included and encouraged. To us, a poem is nothing without its writer and so we tell our writers that we are here to promote their work in any way we can. Rough Diamond is a space where there is belief in the writers and their words.

In the future we hope to put some print anthologies together, as well as doing themed competitions.

*When are your submission windows?*

We aim to publish four times a year— a collection for each season. At the moment we don't have definite, set in stone dates, but constantly update social media and our journal with all the necessary information.

*How should authors go about approaching you with their writing and is there a best practice?*

This is the most difficult question. We know what it is like to send work out and so we don't expect that you've read absolutely everything in our journal — although we'd love it if people did! However, reading the guidelines is definitely the most important thing. For example, we don't accept work in an attachment but still receive many attachments. We always welcome a querying writer and will respond to all questions regarding submitting— there are no stupid questions!

*What are your turnaround times like and do you give unsolicited feedback?*

We try to be as quick as possible when responding to writers. As you can imagine, sometimes life gets in the way and can become difficult. Sometimes we respond to people that very day and other times it may be a few weeks. Always look at our Twitter page— occasionally when we are busy working through submissions we'll get people to submit there and then for a quick response. We also know what it is like to wait and so we don't mind if poets send us an email wondering what is happening with their submission.

*Do you focus on representing particular voices or geographical locations?*

We would love to have a wide range of diverse writers and already have poets featured from all over the world. But when it comes to reading through submissions we never read your biography, or any information about you, until the end. Ultimately, your writing is what's important to us and we choose what speaks or sings to us— because of this, we feel we get a wide range of different people and places in an authentic way.

*Would you expect to see a cover letter from a writer and if so, what would you love to see in it?*

We don't mind a submission with or without a cover letter. We often enjoy a 'hello' and poets telling us what they've been up to but we're equally fine with just your poems and a third person bio. We don't want writers to feel as if they have to sell themselves to us before we consider their work— we want the work to speak for you.

**Website**:

roughdiamondpoetry.com

**Twitter:**

@PoetryRough

**Email:**

roughdiamondpoems@gmail.com

**Editor:** Charlotte Cosgrove

*"Breathe in experience, breathe out poetry."*
Charlotte Cosgrove's first poetry book,
*'Silent Violence with Petals'* will be out in June 2022 with Kelsay Books.

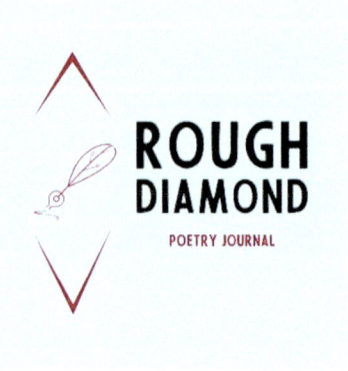

*In Conversation with... Rob Greene, Founder & Publisher*
*Raleigh NC, USA*

**Pay? Y Simultaneous submissions? Y Feedback? Y**
**Online publication? Y Print Publication? Y**

*What is the editorial focus for your literary journal and what have you set out to achieve?*

Raleigh Review is a resourceful, nonprofit magazine of poetry, short fiction, and art, offering accessible works of experience that are emotionally and intellectually complex. At Raleigh Review we believe that great literature inspires empathy by allowing us to see the world through the eyes of our neighbours, whether across the street or across the globe. Our mission is to foster the creation and availability of accessible, yet provocative, contemporary literature. Raleigh Review has fostered the development of two literary magazine-publishing programs, one at Louisburg College, a nearby two-year college, and one at Saint Augustine's University, an HBCU in Raleigh.

*When are your submission windows?*

January 1 to June 1 & July 1 to October 31.

*How should authors go about approaching you with their writing and is there a best practice?*

See our archives and our guidelines at https://www.raleighreview.org/

**Contact Details:**

Raleigh Review, USA - https://www.raleighreview.org/

*In Conversation with… Ann Beman, Co-Owner and Non-Fiction Editor*
*CA, USA*

**Pay? Y Simultaneous submissions? Y Feedback? Y
Online publication? N Print Publication? Y**

*What is the editorial focus for your literary journal and what have you set out to achieve?*

We publish poetry, essays, short stories, flash fiction & flash nonfiction. We're committed to paying the writer and everyone involved in the production of our magazine. To keep the body of work fresh, we'll never solicit: 100% of our work is from the open queue. Finally, to keep writers moving forward, we provide feedback, if requested.

*How should authors go about approaching you with their writing and is there a best practice?*

Visit our Submittable page for the latest TLR submission guidelines. Our Transparency in Publishing has details about how we use submission and subscription fees to pay writers and our support staff. Our excerpts page and Soundcloud channel have examples of what we accept. https://tahomaliteraryreview.com/pages/guidelines

*Do you focus on representing particular voices or geographical locations?*

Promoting diversity is a fundamental goal at Tahoma Literary Review. We strive to attract and promote as many diverse voices as possible. We offer free submissions for marginalized writers.

**Contact Details:**

Contact TLR via our website's contact form: https://tahomaliteraryreview.com/pages/contact

**Pay? N Simultaneous submissions? N Feedback? N
Online publication? Y Print Publication? Y**

*We know that your main focus is poetry but do you ever accept
submissions which verge on cross-genre or which are stylistically different
to the rest of your publishing aesthetic?*

We are happy to consider poetry, short stories and flash fiction, as well as
submissions verging on cross-genre. However, considerations of space mean
that work of more than 2000 words is unlikely to be accommodated.

*What is the editorial focus for your literary journal and what have you
set out to achieve?*

We tend to avoid work that is either very traditional or very experimental,
favouring poetry and prose that falls somewhere in between and yet is
both well-crafted and appropriately challenging for the reader. We believe
our readers should be prepared to do some heavy lifting, but should not
be required to make a disproportionate investment of time or effort to
appreciate the work we publish.

*Do you focus on representing particular voices or geographical locations?*

We receive submissions from all over the world and we are receptive to the
work of writers from different social, cultural and ideological backgrounds.
We are happy to consider work translated from languages other than English
and have published both poetry and prose in translation.

**Contact Details:**

frogmorepress@gmail.com

In Conversation with… Zak Block, founder
Brooklyn, NY, USA

**Pay? N Simultaneous submissions? Y Feedback? Y
Online publication? Y**

*We know that your main focus is poetry, but do you ever accept
submissions which verge on cross-genre or which are stylistically different
to the rest of your publishing aesthetic?*

Yes we do: it's important for writers to continually push genre boundaries,
in the hopes that we can, as a literary culture, recapture the freewheeling
energy of the mid-century American postmodern literature. By which I
mean, not unlike those Shaggy, Crunchy, Braggadocious Lit Brats of the late
90s and early 2000s, so that we end up with something still disingenuous
and hollow but slightly more engaging than infinite Vampire fan-fiction.

*What is the editorial focus for your literary journal and what have you
set out to achieve?*

We attempt to make the editorial 'vibe' that of a 1970s debutante ball,
embodying the spirit of traditional deb culture, but with a seventies sheen
of polyester and tonsorial fluffliness. We encourage contributors to travel
in their minds to that wonderful time and place, and evoke, through the
composition of creative writing and lyrics, the bashful physicalities of the
ball's middle-aged well-wishers in big hats.

*Would you expect to see a cover letter from a writer and if so, what would
you love to see in it?*

People who submit to us tend to write self-effacing cover letters, with
occasional apologies if they've failed to adhere to any submission formalities.

Instead of a traditional cover letter, I would rather see something more creative in an introduction. Help me to get to know you and your work.

**Contact Details:**

climputh@gmail.com

*In Conversation with... Kirsty Allison, Editor*
*London, UK*

**Pay? Y Simultaneous submissions? N Feedback? N**
**Online publication? Y Print Publication? Y**

*We know that your main focus is across poetry, stories and art, but do*
*you ever accept submissions which verge on cross-genre or which are*
*stylistically different to the rest of your publishing aesthetic?*

Ambit was established in 1959. Past editors include JG Ballard, Carol Ann-
Duffy, Eduardo Paolozzi, with early work from David Hockney, Linton
Kwesi Johnson, Ralph Steadman. Some of our most radical works are cross-
disciplinary.

When I came on board, we started using Poems, Stories, Art as a way of
describing Ambit, nodding to the traditions of founder Dr Martin Bax, to
offer thirty pages to each of these disciplines per issue. Traditionally, these
areas have been headed up by separate editors, overseen by one— and in
my mind, progressive literature and art has always occurred where there's
some sort of visionary overlap. I love the Invisible Years series in Ambit,
the collaboration between Ron Sanford, Martin, JG Ballard and occasionally
Mike Foreman. Culture moves, it is alive, and we are undoubtedly
gatekeeping if people want to give it a go— but we are in a very different
point to where we began, because anyone can publish their own work now,
and that was not possible back when we began in 1959.

What we offer is stories on paper, that's the core of Ambit. Ambit is a
platform for publishing the best literature and art, and if someone chose
to submit graphic stories, we'd see it and consider. There are many great
artists, poets and writers that start with us— stories take many forms and
we're here to platform the best poetry, stories and art, but that isn't to
deny cross-over. Our only restriction is that we have ninety-six pages in our
quarterlies where submission is open to all, and we clearly have an intention
with the Annual Ambit Competition, which opened across disciplines for

the first time in 2021, and will this year, with a theme as the framework.

Fiction is one way of telling stories, as is art, graphic art, auto-narratives in illustration, etc. Anecdotes or philosophical questions are where many stories begin, so it's generally about how well they transverse into black and white using language, the semiotics, these elements across disciplines are what we play with. Lifewriting is a spectrum: if you're Bukowski or Anaïs Nin your stories are going to be interesting, and for me, that's what makes a great writer. I had very little to share until I'd lived a bit. It's not about disruption and colour all the time, but it helps if there's some mastery. Form is a tool. Speech is a tool. I love these borderlines— where lyric and poetry crossover has been an obsession.

*"I'm just beginning on Ambit, it's an honour to be defining what Story is. We select on merit and we have a strong history of experimental cross-disciplinary collaborations but most writers will generally specialise in that form.*

*It doesn't matter whether you've been published before in Ambit, or have grand bibliographies, we are demonstrating what contemporary fiction and story is, but that is in no way to delineate the power of classical story. There's comfort in tradition and rules and knowing form rather than swashbuckling through without context, but naïvety in writing will often be potent rather than grey and wise. We're in polemical times, and the breadth of what I've seen so far reflects that."*

Kate Pemberton's last issue is in February 2022, Ambit 246, and interestingly it's all females who are being published. She's been an incredible fiction editor. I've learnt a great deal from her experience. We have conversations about the context of author as artist, but really, all it comes down to is how well the story's told and what it's doing that is original, and why we'd want to go through the process of subbing, using paper, designing, in order to offer it to our readers.

There is an element of instinct to reading. What I've always found with having any critical rubric is there is the magic quotient that lives beyond skill, or it's passé before it's begun. The issue edited by Lias Saoudi of Fat

White Family has a girth of styles from Ben Myers to Rob Doyle, but the next issue, 245, was dedicated to the selections of judges Kim Addonizio and Michael Salu, so there's all sorts of angles there. Even with our Poems, some in the next issue are almost Flash Fiction.

I'm learning as I go, and every selection brings up a more defined context of how culture is curated and created. There is a creative space where fiction and non-fiction cross-over, which is something to explore. I called it Stories rather than Prose or Fiction. It's up to writers, poets and artists to explore this.

It is all in the edit, really, not only for myself, but for the writers. But I am always going to say, a Story can be anything that works on paper for Ambit. Maybe we should say it's Writing and Art. The Writing takes the form of Stories and Poems. The voice doesn't need to shout to be heard, calming narratives are one form, and whispers are fine.

*When are your submission windows?*

Please subscribe to our newsletter and find us on social media for submission and competition dates.

*Would you expect to see a cover letter from a writer and if so, what would you love to see in it?*

Yes we do ask for cover letters, although we often look under the covers before. We're curious. Entertain us.

**Contact Details:**

AMBIT | Support, Subscribe, Submit | https://ambitmagazine.co.uk | contact@ambitmagazine.co.uk | +447835 227 065 | London office (for general correspondence): 35 Holly Grove, Peckham, London, SE15 5DF | Norfolk HQ: Staithe House, Main Road, Brancaster Staithe, Norfolk, PE31 8BP

**FLASHBACK FICTION**

*In Conversation with... Ingrid Jendrzejewski, Editor in Chief*
*Cambridge, UK*

**Pay? N Simultaneous submissions? Y Feedback? N
Online publication? Y Print Publication? N**

*We know that your main focus is flash fiction, but do you ever accept submissions which verge on cross-genre or which are stylistically different to the rest of your publishing aesthetic?*

FlashBack Fiction aims to celebrate historical shortform work in all forms — flash fiction, prose poetry and hybrid; traditional and experimental. We welcome 'hermit crabs', micros, and unclassifiable work and actively encourage writers to experiment and play. Pieces that look and feel like poetry of the non-prose variety are unlikely to find a place with us, though feel free to try us with anything on the boundaries. The only absolute requirement is that the piece engages with history in some way and is 500 words or fewer. (We have no minimum word count and welcome super short submissions.)

*What is the editorial focus for your literary journal and what have you set out to achieve?*

FlashBack Fiction is an online journal publishing one historical shortform piece per week during our publishing seasons. We accompany each piece with audio, and a follow-up interview with the author.

We don't have a strict cut-off date for what we consider 'history', but pieces set after 2000 are a harder sell, as are memoir-style pieces with a contemporary narrator looking back on their life. ('Harder' does not mean 'impossible'.)

We're particularly interested in pieces that fill gaps in the history books. We welcome stories from around the world, and from writers of all backgrounds.

*What are your turnaround times like and do you give unsolicited feedback?*

We are slow, aiming to reply within two to four months. Every submission is read by at least three editors, and the entire team reads and discusses every submission that makes it through the first reading. We often research the history underpinning a submission before an acceptance.

We occasionally offer feedback when a piece is close or we particularly admire a certain aspect, but welcome authors to tell us in their cover letter if they don't want feedback. We often send along small editorial notes after acceptance, though it is up to the author whether to implement these.

**Contact Details:**

FlashBack Fiction  Website: http://flashbackfiction.com/

Email: flashbackfiction@gmail.com

Twitter: @FlashBackFic

Facebook: https://www.facebook.com/FlashBackFic/

*In Conversation with... Charlie Baylis, Editor*
*Nottingham, UK*

**Pay? N Simultaneous submissions? Y Feedback? N
Online publication? Y**

*What is the editorial focus for your literary journal and what have you set out to achieve?*

Our aim is simply to publish fun, fresh and exciting poems.

We're open to any form or style of poetry: if we like it, we'll publish it. As suggested by our name, we are interested in environmental/eco-poetry but we're not limited to it. We love publishing poets from around the world, wherever you are, get in touch, we're looking forward to hearing from you. We also publish translations from any language (into English).

*What are your turnaround times like and do you give unsolicited feedback?*

For free submissions we aim to get back to you within two months. There is also the option of expedited submissions where you can pay £3 for a 72-Hour response or, if you're desperate to hear back soon, £10 for a 24-hour response. These expedited submission help keep the journal afloat, so we're very grateful for any we receive.

*Would you expect to see a cover letter from a writer and if so, what would you love to see in it?*

Don't put too much effort into the cover letter, we're much more interested in the poems...

**Contact Details:**

https://www.anthropocenepoetry.org/ - anthropocenepoetry@gmail.com

*In Conversation with... Isabelle Kenyon, Editor*
*Manchester, UK*

**Pay? Y Simultaneous submissions? Y Feedback? N**
**Online publication? Y Print Publication? Y**

*We know that your main focus is on poetry and flash fiction, but do you ever accept submissions which verge on cross-genre or which are stylistically different to the rest of your publishing aesthetic?*

We are happy to accept submissions with merge across genres— and equally open to new forms. For example, in our Food magazine, we published Sam J Grudgings' poetry, which featured footnotes as poems in themselves. We love to see innovation in this way. There should be no rules in creative writing!

*What is the editorial focus for your literary journal and what have you set out to achieve?*

Fly on the Wall Press aims to be ethical, sustainable and accessible. This applies to our communication with writers and readers (open, honest, friendly), our pay standards and our FSC certified paper, carbon-neutral and recycled book packaging — we never use plastic. We even have plant starch *Sellotape*! Our journal is themed per issue. In the past, we have had Power, Food, Unite and Alien.

*When are your submission windows?*

Typically once or twice a year with updates at: https://www. flyonthewallpress.co.uk/magazine-guidelines

*How should authors go about approaching you with their writing and is there a best practice?*

Only send an email when our submissions window is open for the magazine and do tell us a bit about you - a few lines will do! This is especially important if you are submitting your work to us for the first time. We'd really appreciate it if you had read a past issue of our magazine, to support our writers.

## What are your turnaround times like and do you give unsolicited feedback?

We get back to everyone within five weeks' time and we sometimes do offer a line or so of feedback, particularly to indicate which pieces we liked best.

**Contact Details:**

flyonthewallpress@hotmail.com

**Political. Ethical. Sustainable. A publisher with a conscience.**

 The British Book Awards 2021

**Small Press of the Year**

REGIONAL FINALIST

#BRITISHBOOKAWARDS

*In Conversation with... Rowan Bagley, Editor in Chief*
VT, USA

**Pay? N Simultaneous submissions? Y Feedback? Y
Online publication? Y Print Publication? N**

*We know that you publish the genres of poetry, short stories and flash
fiction, but do you ever accept submissions which verge on cross-genre or
which are stylistically different to the rest of your publishing aesthetic?*

We don't necessarily have a main focus in terms of poetry vs. short story vs.
flash and we enjoy seeing work that crosses or blends mediums. We tend to
publish things that are darkly atmospheric and haunting. We understand that
can come in many forms, which is all the more reason to leave our theme
somewhat broad. We don't want anyone to feel limited by our aesthetic.

*What is the editorial focus for your literary journal and what have you
set out to achieve?*

Our focus is to give a platform to marginalized artists who create in the
horror and surrealism genres. Horror is a white, cis, male-dominated genre
and we saw the need for a space that prioritizes work in that genre from
people who have been historically ostrocized in horror-loving spaces.

*When are your submission windows?*

We take submissions on a rolling basis, but go on hiatus from November 1st
- January 1st to work on our yearly anthology.

*How should authors go about approaching you with their writing and is
there a best practice?*

We're very casual, open people at Not Deer and we don't expect our
contributors to be overly formal. Best practice is to approach us with
enthusiasm and transparency, always tell us if your work comes with a

content warning or has been published elsewhere in the past, for example, as that's the energy we'll be giving you.

*What are your turnaround times like and do you give unsolicited feedback?*

Our turnaround is typically less than two weeks, although it can be more depending on what else is going on in our lives. If turnaround times go beyond two weeks, we email submitters to let them know. We don't give unsolicited feedback, but anyone can request feedback for a small fee (typically $3-$5).

*Do you focus on representing particular voices or geographical locations?*

We focus on representing work from BIPOC, women, LGBT+, disabled, and international voices, as we feel they are underrepresented in the genre we specialise in.

*Would you expect to see a cover letter from a writer and if so, what would you love to see in it?*

We don't expect to see cover letters, we only ask for a short and engaging biography. We love to see fun facts about submitters, where we can find more of their work, and what they do in their spare time.

## NOT DEER MAGAZINE

# AN ART AND LITERATURE MAGAZINE FOR THE HORRIFIC AND SURREAL

Founded in 2021 by Editor-in-Chief Rowan Bagley, Not Deer Magazine specializes in publishing work from marginalized creators who are often overlooked as part of the horror genre.
Our goal is to be part of the shifting dynamics in literary circles and offer alternative perspectives in a genre that has been historically white male-dominated.
Our published works are available to read on our magazine website. We hope you give us a visit.

# Top 5 Tips for Submitting to *Not Deer Magazine*

1.       <u>Read submission guidelines thoroughly.</u> We pride ourselves on the transparency and thoughtfulness we put into our guidelines page because we don't want potential contributors to be confused by what we're asking for, but as a submitter we ask that you do your part by reading them. We're always more than happy to answer questions if we haven't been clear about something!

2.       <u>Take a look at our previously published work before submitting.</u> We don't have a specific theme here at *Not Deer* unless we're doing a contest, but we do tend to lean more toward atmospheric and haunting literature above everything else and most of our published work reflects these aesthetic preferences.

3.       <u>Make sure your work has been heavily edited beforehand.</u> There's nothing that takes us out of a piece more than repeated spelling, grammar, and clarity errors, so we ask our submitters to go over their work with a fine-toothed comb before sending it to us. In the future we may offer editing workshops, but we can't offer those intensive services to every piece that comes to our inbox.

4.       <u>Tell the story you want to tell, not the one you think we want to hear.</u> We love originality. We love seeing work that challenges us and gets its claws stuck in our mind. Nothing does this to us more than work that comes from the gut, work that begs you to see it through to the end. We want your gut stories, not your fluff.

5.       <u>Never take a rejection personally.</u> We love reading everything and anything you send us, but we can't accept all of it. That has nothing to do with your skill as an artist or our feelings about you as a person and we promise we want to hear from you again. We love you and you give us life.

**Contact Details**

Contact us at notdeermag@gmail.com,

notdeermagazine.com,

or on Twitter @NotDeerMag

*In Conversation with… Carolina VonKampen, Editor in Chief*
MO, USA

**Pay? N Simultaneous submissions? Y Feedback? N
Online publication? Y Print Publication? Y**

*What is the editorial focus for your literary journal and what have you set out to achieve?*

Our print literary magazine publishes once each season, and our goal is to capture a specific feeling or mood that we experience in that season. We have a penchant for pretty words, an affinity to the melancholy, and an an undeniably time-ful aura. We believe that stories exist in a specific moment, and that that moment is what makes stories unique. Words stay with us as we go through life, and the words we kept sacred yesterday may be different than the words we need today. We are here to give them to you, one season at a time.

*When are your submission windows?*

We are open year-round for print edition submissions, and the submission theme changes every three months or so. Our print edition themes are closely tied to each season, and we're looking for stories, poems, and essays that weave the season and theme together. Our blog submissions are open year-round with no deadlines, and we're interested in essays that talk about reading the right book at the right time or the intersection of your reading life with writing or traveling.

*Would you expect to see a cover letter from a writer and if so, what would you love to see in it?*

In a cover letter, we want to see five things:

- What category your submission is (poetry, story, essay)

- Confirmation the submission has not been published anywhere else

- Your full name

- Your bio

- Your pronouns (if not included in your bio)

Although it's not necessary, writers might also like to include:

- Title(s) of the story, essay, or poem(s) you're submitting

- If the submission is a simultaneous submission

- What the story, poem(s), or essay is about/what inspired you to write it

- How you found out about *Capsule Stories*

- Your social media handles

**Contact Details:**

CapsuleStories.com

Instagram: @CapsuleStoriesMag

Twitter and Facebook: @CapsuleStories

*In Conversation with... Henry Bell, Editor*
*Glasgow, Scotland, UK*

**Pay? Y Simultaneous submissions? N Feedback? N**
**Print Publication? Y**

*What is the editorial focus for your literary journal and what have you set out to achieve?*

We're always excited by work that pushes boundaries, and whilst we tend to divide what we print into poetry, fiction and non-fiction, things that push at the edges of those forms and subvert our editors expectations are always a delight.

*When are your submission windows?*

Our submissions window opens each August and February for around five weeks.

*Do you focus on representing particular voices or geographical locations?*

We're interested in new Scottish writing, but within an international context. So while preference is given to writers from or with a connection to Scotland we also publish work from around the globe in each issue.

**Contact Details:**

contactguttermagazine@gmail.com

*In Conversation with... Leia, Head Editor*
*Ilford, UK*

**Pay? N Simultaneous submissions? Y Feedback? Y
Online Publication? Y Print Publication? Y**

*We know that your main focus is on poetry and flash fiction, but do you ever accept submissions which verge on cross-genre or which are stylistically different to the rest of your publishing aesthetic?*

We accept submissions across a variety of different genres, including artwork, but especially love submissions with an experimental edge. We do not have specific criteria or one particular style of pieces that we publish genre/style wise. As long as the piece is bold, confident, and well-constructed, we'll be very happy to consider it. Our current limit for prose is 750 words due to space constraints with issue size, but we may review this in 2022.

*What is the editorial focus for your literary journal and what have you set out to achieve?*

The editorial focus of our journal is to showcase fantastic writers who deserve recognition for their wonderful creations. We aim to be a home for all voices and provide a space where writing is celebrated, and writers are supported. We have a diverse team of volunteer readers and also welcome Guest Editors for each issue — specifically emerging writers from the Global South.

*When are your submission windows?*

We ask for submissions at four main points across the year, and our next open windows for the second half of 2022 are the following:

20th July- subs open; 10th August- subs close.

*How should authors go about approaching you with their writing and is there a best practice?*

Writers can submit their work to us via a google form on our website. Best practice with our journal is simply to read the guidelines! We are also very grateful when writers or creators let us know when their submission has been accepted elsewhere. We are always happy to answer any questions that writers or creators have, so if you are unsure of anything, don't hesitate to let us know!

*What are your turnaround times like and do you give unsolicited feedback?*

We aim to get back to authors with an answer within one month after the submission closing date. We offer the option to all submitters to select if they would like free feedback with their submission with the understanding that the feedback could take up to six months (this will not impact our initial answer regarding their submission, the feedback will come later separately).

*Do you focus on representing particular voices or geographical locations?*

Our main focus is to simply welcome as many voices as possible, no limitations on this as long as our guidelines are followed!

*Would you expect to see a cover letter from a writer and if so, what would you love to see in it?*

We accept submissions through a google form, so no cover letter is required. We always welcome writers and creators reaching out to say hi, ask a question, or let us know if their submission has been accepted elsewhere. We also have space on our submission form so that writers and creators can tell us why they wrote their submission and tell us a little about the piece!

**Contact Details:**

Head Editors - Leia Butler and JP Seabright

Email- fullhouselitmag@gmail.com

Twitter- @fullhouselit, Instagram- fullhouselitmag

Website- https://www.fullhouseliterary.com/

A hello from

# FULL HOUSE

SUBMIT to our issues

feature on our PODCAST

READ or write a review

view our free WORKSHOP

Join the FH family

GET IN TOUCH

WWW.FULLHOUSELITMAG.COM

@fullhouselitmag @fullhouselit

*In Conversation with… Helen Ivory, Editor in Chief*
*Norwich, UK*

**Pay? N Simultaneous submissions? N Feedback? N
Online Publication? Y Print Publications? Y**

*We know that your main focus is poetry, but do you ever accept submissions which verge on cross-genre or which are stylistically different to the rest of your publishing aesthetic?*

A benefit of being an online publication is we can feature Word and Image work and Filmpoems as well as traditional-looking poems and prose. For the latter, we have a word limit of 750 words, so you can see the whole piece with as little scrolling as possible. We celebrate many exciting mixed-media, wide-ranging modes of creativity.

Our print publications also push boundaries. We occasionally commission new work; past winners include Jay Bernard and Gail McConnell. We work on special projects, such as Runaways London in conjunction with Spread the Word and the University of Glasgow's Runaway Slaves in Britain project.

*What is the editorial focus for your literary journal and what have you set out to achieve?*

We have eclectic, magpie-like tastes and so our focus is all-of-the-things. We only ask that they are shiny and speak to us. We like well-made things; we like things made by up-and-coming writers who are finding their feet as creative practitioners. We love hearing: *'IS&T was the first place to publish me seven years ago'*, from a writer who has since gone on to publish a full collection of poems, for example. We are a platform for new work and have always aimed to publish diverse voices.

*When are your submission windows?*

Generally, our editing interns are open for submissions from the 1-15th of each month and chief editor Helen Ivory from the 16th to the month's end, but this can change due to the volumes we receive. Word and Image and Filmpoems should always be submitted to IS&T interns and we also have dedicated submission windows for our National Poetry Day and Twelve Days of Christmas features. Details can be found at https://inksweatandtears.co.uk/submissions/

We ask that authors read the submission guidelines on the site and then just send us a nice note when they submit their work. The submission guidelines are there to save everybody time on administrative tasks. (Having to write to the author requesting their biography is an extra administrative task, for example.)

*What are your turnaround times like and do you give unsolicited feedback?*

We normally try to get back to people, either way, within eight weeks, though sometimes it is much less. We do not give unsolicited feedback. We believe that feedback is more effective in a creative writing class, workshop or poetry surgery. Helen (Ivory) teaches creative writing, and keeps her feedback brain for that.

*Do you focus on representing particular voices or geographical locations?*

The aim is to represent the entire English-speaking world and we also welcome translations into English from the rest of the world. This is a huge aim but is nonetheless sincere. In January 2021, we began an editing internship programme. IS&T internships run for four months each consecutively, and in order to go some way towards redressing the balance in publishing, will for the foreseeable future come from the Black, Asian, Latinx and other ethnic minority communities within the UK. Our interns have included Memoona Zahid, Fahad Al-Amoudi, Desree and Leah Jun Oh.

*Would you expect to see a cover letter from a writer and if so, what would you love to see in it?*

A short covering email is always nice, as it makes the whole thing feel like a human transaction rather than somebody just batting their work over a fence at you. Something simple, like: 'Dear _____ I'd be grateful/ delighted/ pleased if you consider the attached works for publication on IS&T. They are not under consideration elsewhere. I have also attached a short bio. Thank you for your time.' That would work. It's succinct and courteous.

## Contact Details:

We only accept submissions by email, during submissions windows which can be found on our Submissions Page (https://inksweatandtears.co.uk/submissions/) and are announced on social media

To submit work to editor Helen Ivory, email: inksweatandtearssubmissions@gmail.com

To submit to the editing intern, email: inksweatandtearsinterns@gmail.com.

In Conversation with... Rebecca Moon Ruark, Features Editor
VA, USA

**Pay? N Simultaneous submissions? Y Feedback? Y
Online Publication? Y**

*We know that your main focus is on genres poetry, short stories and flash fiction, but do you ever accept submissions which verge on cross-genre or which are stylistically different to the rest of your publishing aesthetic?*

Parhelion Literary Magazine offers bold literature for bold readers. Presently, we consider poetry, short stories, and flash fiction for our issues. We also publish features on a rolling basis. Features can be essays on the writing life, satirical takes on life-right-now, book reviews, or author interviews; we're especially interested in highlighting recent publications from smaller or independent presses. As far as aesthetic, while much of what we publish falls into the literary category, we take our hair down for our yearly Halloween issue, which features horror, suspense, and more to keep you up all night.

*What is the editorial focus for your literary journal and what have you set out to achieve?*

Parhelion champions all writers, but it's our passion to discover promising and bright new voices out there. We've been fortunate to have high school age interns assist with reading submissions, and their insights help us keep our triannual issues fresh. For more editorial direction, be sure to check us out on Submittable.

*Do you focus on representing particular voices or geographical locations?*

Yes and no. Our journal is headquartered in Richmond, Virginia, in the American South. We love our complicated and diverse home and love to feature writers who help us parse the complexities of the South. But we're more than regional. We're read by an international audience and encourage submissions in English from international poets and writers. We seek skilful, fearless writing from all comers!

**Contact Details:**

parhelionliterary.com; parhelionlit@gmail.com

*In Conversation with... Dawn Bauling, Editor*
*Devon, UK*

**Pay? N Simultaneous submissions? N Feedback? Y
Print Publication? Y**

*We know that your main focus is poetry, but do you ever accept submissions which verge on cross-genre or which are stylistically different to the rest of your publishing aesthetic?*

For Sarasvati we consider any genre and any style, whether poetry or prose. It's an experimental magazine that showcases an author's work, so that's the focus. For The Dawntreader we consider poetry and prose with the themes of nature, myth, legend and spirituality, love and the environment and we do stick to that to preserve the flavour of the magazine.

*What is the editorial focus for your literary journal and what have you set out to achieve?*

With Sarasvati we want people to showcase their work to show a breadth of styles and experience. Each issue should be a snapshot of what's happening internationally in writing communities. With The Dawntreader we want to provide escape and calm, a soothing celebration of the natural and supernatural world, the inner and outer person. With both magazines we want to forge a community of mutually supportive writers that learns from the pooled wisdom and shared interest.

*When are your submission windows?*

All year round for both magazines.

*How should authors go about approaching you with their writing and is there a best practice?*

Email submissions to me at dawnidp@gmail.com — prose up to 1000 words and up to four poems of roughly 30-40 lines.

*What are your turnaround times like and do you give unsolicited feedback?*

We try to give a response in 48 hours but, at busy times, it can be more. We let authors know if there is a holiday or a longer wait time for a response. We occasionally give some feedback if work needs only a small tweak to enable it to be accepted.

*Do you focus on representing particular voices or geographical locations?*

No — quality is the only measure for accepting work. We have a fully international subscriber and contributor base.

*Would you expect to see a cover letter from a writer and if so, what would you love to see in it?*

Yes — we consider it a courtesy. Emails with just an attachment are not opened. We only ask for a name and an address so we can send on a copy of the issue successful writers are in. It's always good to know that a writer knows who you are before sending AND gets your name right. It shows how serious and interested they are about a magazine, rather than just being published.

**SARASVATI,** a quarterly magazine, showcases poetry and prose, with each successful contributor having 3-4 A5 pages dedicated to their work.

Submit up to 4 poems or prose (to 1,000 words) sent as email attachments, along with a brief 2-3 line bio to go with the pieces and a postal address. Please note: as a courtesy submissions must have a covering note otherwise they will be deleted.

If relevant, we publish details of the collection/book the work is taken from and how to buy. All styles considered, submissions by email preferred.

**THE DAWNTREADER** quarterly is our highest circulation magazine. It has an international readership which gives the opportunity to let the imagination run free. The Dawntreader specialises in the themes: myth, legend; in the landscape, nature; spirituality and love; the mystic, the environment. It fulfils a niche in the market, welcoming poetry, prose, articles and local legends.

**Editor Dawn Bauling:**
**Winner of the Ted Slade Award for Services to Poetry**
*Most Innovative Publisher 2021*

**Best Collaborative Work Award 2021** *Forest, moor or less*

**Prices for both magazines:**

**UK £4.50 per issue,**

**£17 four issue subscription**

**Overseas £7 per issue,**

**£26 four issue subscription**

www.indigodreamspublishing.com

@IndigoDreamsPub

**Contact Details:**
The Dawntreader;Sarasvati Magazine,
Indigo Dreams Publishing,
24, Forest Houses, Halwill,
Beaworthy, Devon, EX21 5UU

*In Conversation with... Raef Boylan, Chief Editor*
*Coventry, UK*

**Pay? N Simultaneous submissions? Y Feedback? Y**
**Online Publication? Y Print Publication? Y**

*What is the editorial focus for your literary journal and what have you set out to achieve?*

Our overall aim is pretty simple: to showcase a lively but accessible selection of high-quality writing and art that both enthrals and entertains. Well-crafted, thought-provoking, exploring the theme in an original way — all that good stuff. HCE is a community-minded platform (which is why our logo is a group of ants working together to achieve a goal!) so we're equally as excited to be somebody's first publishing credit as when we receive submissions from illustrious names. What's important is giving creatives a boost, by producing a magazine they're proud to be featured in and that other people want to read.

*How should authors go about approaching you with their writing and is there a best practice?*

Work must be sent via the form on our website (not by email) while the HCE submissions window is open. All pieces should connect with the respective theme, but we choose multi-faceted themes and welcome innovative interpretations. If your link to the theme isn't transparent, please provide some context. We dislike receiving pieces that use our exact theme as their title; repetitive headings would put the magazine at risk of feeling monotonous. Please refer to our guidelines for requirements such as word counts. Unpublished work is preferred, but we currently accept simultaneous submissions/pieces that have previously appeared elsewhere.

*Would you expect to see a cover letter from a writer and if so, what would you love to see in it?*

We prefer a short cover letter and biography. Bare minimum: let us know why you think HCE is a good home for your writing. HCE has a diverse, global readership, so it's good to include geographical location and some personal background info. (We only look at bios after reading the submission itself, to avoid pre-judgments). Sometimes we receive full, lengthy CVs —please don't do this to us! It's best to select only a handful of your publication credits/achievements to tell us about. We list contributor biographies online, so you're welcome to include a social media handle and website link.

**Contact Details:**

Website: https://hcemagazine.com

Facebook: @HCEmagazine

Twitter: @HereComesEvery1

Instagram: @hce_magazine

Email: raef@hcemagazine.com

*In Conversation with... Roger Bloor Co-Editor*
*Newcastle Staffs, UK*

**Pay? N Simultaneous submissions?  Y Feedback?  N
Online Publication?  Y Print Publication?  Y**

*What is the editorial focus for your literary journal and what have you
set out to achieve?*

The Alchemy Spoon is a platform for poetry without prejudice especially
of race, gender or age. We are particularly interested to invite poems from
'new phase poets'. These are poets who have come late to poetry, often
following retirement, or a life-change.

The work of new phase poets often has stunning depth and perspective
reflecting experiences accumulated from work and life. These poets
might be classed among those who have been dubbed the 'lost generation
of talent'. Abid Hussain, Diversity Director at the AHRC (Arts and
Humanities Research Council), says: "How many would-be working-class
artists, artistic directors, choreographers, composers and curators decided
to enter accounting, legal, medical and engineering professions instead?"

The Alchemy Spoon aims to demonstrate that this talent was not lost but
waiting for a reappraisal of priorities, an unleashing of latent creativity,
waiting for its time.

*How should authors go about approaching you with their writing and is
there a best practice?*

We use the Dousuma submission system from Doutrope which can be
accessed through our website or direct at Doutrope.

*What are your turnaround times like and do you give unsolicited feedback?*

We respond to all submissions within four weeks of the end of the submission window, whilst we don't give detailed feedback we do inform any shortlisted poets not selected for publication which poem we shortlisted.

**Contact Details:**

By email at alchemyspoon@btinternet.com or via our contact page on alchemyspoon.org

# SHOOTER LITERARY MAGAZINE

*In Conversation with... Melanie White, Editor/Publisher*
*Cheltenham, UK*

**Pay? Y Simultaneous submissions? Y Feedback? N**
**Online Publication? Y Print Publication? Y**

*When are your submission windows?*

We accept short fiction, nonfiction and poetry September-November for the winter issue and February-April for the summer issue, but we also accept flash fiction/nonfiction on a rolling basis for our monthly Shooter Flash showcase. Shooter's annual Short Story Competition is open February-May, and the annual Poetry Competition is open August-November. Please visit the website at https://shooterlitmag.com for guidelines and further details!

*How should authors go about approaching you with their writing and is there a best practice?*

It should go without saying, but writers should always read and adhere to the guidelines posted on the website before submitting their work. Writers who have read the magazine and familiarised themselves with the kind of literary fare we publish also give themselves the best chance of success. There's no need for lengthy cover letters or summaries. All we care about is the quality of the work: compelling, engaging, well written stories and poems that appeal to both the head and the heart.

*What are your turnaround times like and do you give unsolicited feedback?*

We usually send acceptances within a few weeks of the deadline, while all other writers can expect to hear around a month later. Those who appreciate swift responses might like Shooter Flash, which publishes on the second Monday of each month — so all writers who submit their work during the previous month will hear back by that date.

If a writer comes close to acceptance, we do send specific feedback and encouragement to try again. Any writer who wants to buy detailed feedback and a thorough line-edit can do so via Shooter's editing services: https://shooterlitmag.com/editing-services.

**Contact Details:**

General queries: Email shooterlitmag@gmail.com

Website: https://shooterlitmag.com

Twitter: https://twitter.com/ShooterLitMag

Instagram: https://www.instagram.com/ShooterLitMag

Facebook: https://www.facebook.com/ShooterLiteraryMagazine

*In Conversation with... Carolyn Hashimoto Founder and EIC
Dumfries and Galloway, UK*

**Pay? N Simultaneous submissions? Y Feedback? N
Online Publication? Y**

*What genres are your main focus, and do you ever accept submissions
which verge on cross-genre or which are stylistically different to the rest of
your publishing aesthetic?*

All forms of writing are welcome: poetry, prose, creative non-fiction, essay
(lyrical, personal, experimental), hybrid forms as well as visual art and
photography.

*What is the editorial focus for your literary journal and what have you
set out to achieve?*

Skirting Around looks at the politics of women's clothing through creative
writing and visual art. It is a platform for writers and artists to examine the
political, social, cultural, and emotion issues that are embedded in women's
clothes and bodies. As the title suggests, we are looking for work that dares
to explore topics that are too often skirted around but are inherently linked
to women's clothing and the female body: body shaming, sexism, rape
culture, transgender issues, religious clothing, and clothing that has been
banned.

*When are your submission windows?*

We publish online twice a year in Spring and Autumn. Dates for submissions
are posted on the website.

**Contact Details:**

Website: www.skirtingaround.org   Submissions and enquiries to Carolyn
Hashimoto (Editor in Chief) skirting.around@yahoo.com

*In Conversation with… George Jenkins, Editor*
*Manchester, UK*

**Pay? N Simultaneous submissions? N Feedback? Y**
**Print Publication? Y**

*We know that your main focus is poetry, but do you ever accept submissions which verge on cross-genre or which are stylistically different to the rest of your publishing aesthetic?*

We actively encourage new styles of expression, both in form and content. The consistency of our publication comes through our aesthetic, each page with a 'house styled' collage, and our general D.I.Y. approach. This gives us more freedom with our content meaning we can include, and people expect, a variety of content. We have had many submissions where people have expressed that they would like to submit a piece either to trial it as a new style for them, or because it has been rejected from more standard publications as it deviates from their usual work. We very much enjoy hosting a place where people are free to experiment with these new styles and genres.

*What is the editorial focus for your literary journal and what have you set out to achieve?*

Broadly, we focus on counterculture and any literary piece that represents it. We wanted to produce something that both highlights the work of local writers that may not be used to having work published and make this easily accessible, beyond those already interested. To do this we print the magazine cheaply and sell it cheaply — for just £1. We also try and sell it in places where people might be interested but not normally exposed to small, local, alternative literature (such as record shops and music venues).

*How should authors go about approaching you with their writing and is there a best practice?*

A luxury of being a very small publication is that we are able to stay in quite close contact with writers. We find it best when people approach us casually, either through social media or via email. Having these kind of open communications means we can have good relationships with regular contributors and set new contributors at ease. Their work can then become more closely part of a discussion and involve writers more sincerely with the publication.

**Contact Details:**

Email: simplyupyours@gmail.com

Instagram: @simply_up_yours

*In Conversation with… Georgia Tindale, Co-Founder & Arts Co-Editor*
*Lancaster, UK*

**Pay? N Simultaneous submissions? Y Feedback? N**
**Online Publication? Y Print Publication? Y**

*What is the editorial focus for your literary journal and what have you set out to achieve?*

Founded in 2016, Porridge publishes work across genres, styles and mediums from contributors all around the world. Whether it is poetry, short stories, essays, artwork, photography, videos, creative non-fiction or our popular 'Comfort Foods' series, Porridge aims to showcase diverse, interesting and thought-provoking pieces both online and in print, bringing together international contributors and allowing them to 'speak' to one another through their work. This is especially true of our print magazine, which is open for submissions biannually, and is now on its sixth issue.

*When are your submission windows?*

We open for online submissions in October and April each year and for our printed edition biannually, with rolling submissions for online non-fiction. See the 'Submissions' section of the Porridge website for more information.

*How should authors go about approaching you with their writing and is there a best practice?*

We love it when people approach us who know a little bit about the kind of work we publish (and have read and followed our submissions guidelines!). A 'hello' or another polite address is always welcome when you send us something, and it's helpful to get the editors' names right. I will never forget being addressed as Georgia Tinder in one particularly memorable example!

**Contact Details:** porridgemagazine.com, porridgemagazine@gmail.com

*In Conversation with… Elizabeth Gibson, Editor / Photographer*
*Manchester, UK*

**Pay? N Simultaneous submissions? Y Feedback?  N**
**Online Publication? Y**

*What is the editorial focus for your literary journal and what have you set out to achieve?*

I started Foxglove in 2016, and have lived in three different countries while editing it. My vision has always been to showcase writing that I love, that I find accessible and authentic, and that offers a new look at the world. I pair each piece of writing with a photograph I have taken, and this is a key part of what makes Foxglove what it is. Sometimes, the combinations surprise me, which makes me happy. I am really pleased with where we are now with the journal, five years later.

*How should authors go about approaching you with their writing and is there a best practice?*

We announce submission windows on our website and on Twitter (@ journalfoxglove). Submissions can be sent either by email or using the form on the website, and we ask that writers research Foxglove and send a personalised cover letter explaining why they would like to be part of it. I try to keep bureaucracy and rules to a minimum - I just ask for respect and friendliness, some of your best work, and a genuine interest in the journal.

*Do you focus on representing particular voices or geographical locations?*

From the beginning (when I was living in France), we have attracted a high percentage of international submissions, which I love, and we have published writers from Ireland, Italy, Portugal, Serbia, Zambia, India, Australia, Canada and Mexico, as well as from across the UK and US. I love learning about people's lives and stories in very different places. As a member of the queer community, I would love to receive more poems and stories with queer themes. When I read one, I always have a lovely moment of realisation, and then feel a sense of connection.

**Contact Details:**

grizonne@gmail.com

for submissions or queries.

**Website:**

https://foxglovejournal.wordpress.com.

Twitter: @journalfoxglove

In Conversation with... Patricia McCarthy, Editor and trustee
East Sussex , UK

**Pay? N Simultaneous submissions? N Feedback? Y**
**Print Publication? Y Online Publication? Y**

*We know that your main focus is poetry, but do you ever accept submissions which verge on cross-genre or which are stylistically different to the rest of your publishing aesthetic?*

Agenda is a poetry journal— poems, essays, reviews— occasionally poetic prose.

*What is the editorial focus for your literary journal and what have you set out to achieve?*

To encourage poetry that matters as a vital, living force that cannot be done without. We promote established, little known and new voices (and young poets in the online Broadsheets, with two chosen to appear in the printed journal). Agenda pays no respect to fads or fashion which are ephemeral. We also publish special issues on poets we consider undeservedly neglected, and international issues.

*When are your submission windows?*

These vary (see website).

*How should authors go about approaching you with their writing— is there a best practice?*

We accept only online previously unpublished submissions, each poem on a word doc and a separate brief biography on a word doc. Reviews/ essays need to be approved by the editor at their onset.It is advisable to get hold of a few copies of Agenda (in a library or buy a copy, or, even better, subscribe) before submitting. We like musical poems with interesting imagery that give a tingle down the back when read. We do not like poems that seem written as an unnecessary exercise, or are like mere diary entries. Potential poets would be advised to look at our web supplements online and also to browse the ongoing series 'Notes for Broadsheet Poets' for aspiring poets and their mentors both online and in the printed journal.

*What are your turnaround times like and do you give unsolicited feedback?*

Turnaround times vary depending on the volume of submissions. Feedback is given to subscribers. We say on the website that if you don't hear from us after three months, you can presume your submission is unsuccessful (occasionally the turnaround time is longer).

*Do you focus on representing particular voices or geographical locations?*

We focus on gifted voices from every sector of society, every gender or transgender, and from around the world. We also have special translation issues, and often include translations in each journal. Special international issues occur every so often which gives audiences a wider scope to enjoy poetry and brings to the audience poets they might otherwise not have heard of.

*Would you expect to see a cover letter from a writer and if so, what would you love to see in it?*

No, I don't like cover letters, but I do insist on a brief biography on a word doc (maximum 9 lines, third person, starting with the name, names of books and journals in italics).

## Contact Details:

Agenda poetry journal, Harts Cottage, Stonehurst Lane, Five Ashes, Mayfield, East Sussex. Editor: Patricia McCarthy editor@agendapoetry.co.uk

Admin manager: Marcus Frederick admin@agendapoetry.co.uk

Website www.agendapoetry.co.uk

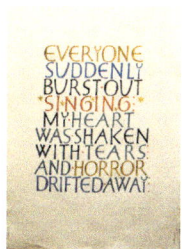

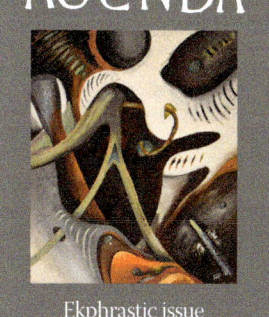

*In Conversation with… Dr Charley Barnes*
*Worcester, UK*

**Pay? N Simultaneous submissions? N Feedback? Y
Print Publication? N Online Publication? Y**

*We know that your main focus is poetry, but do you ever accept submissions which verge on cross-genre or which are stylistically different to the rest of your publishing aesthetic?*

Dear Reader was coined as a poetry journal first and foremost, which has been upheld for some time now in terms of what our publishing focus is. However, in the later stages of 2021, Talis - my brilliant co-editor - and I had a conversation about expanding the focus of the website, which means we now accept submissions of flash fiction as well as reviews. In terms of cross-genre or stylistic experimentation, Talis and I are both suckers for works that surprise us; we love something that looks to be pushing boundaries, or collapsing forms of writing together. We're always open to see work from poets and authors who are looking for ways to re-invent, distort or revive form. Though we don't have see anything wrong with more "traditional" works either, providing the content is sound.

*When are your submission windows?*

Dear Reader is always open for submissions. Our guidelines are available on the website - dearreaderpoetry.com - and there you'll see that we accept submissions all year round. If there's ever a change to that, for any reason, we'll share news of it on our social media channels and on the website's submissions page.

*What are your turnaround times like and do you give unsolicited feedback?*

Talis and I aim to respond to all submissions with 6 weeks of receipt. There are times when there may be a slight delay in this, but this is more to do with us being able to find mutual free time in our diaries than it is to do with anything else! If poets or authors are ever concerned about the length of time we're taking to review their work, they're encouraged to email us again (we really don't mind a nudge, though people should wait for the 6 weeks to pass before they do that). In terms of feedback, we don't typically offer it - meaning, we don't offer it on every piece. However, there have been times when we've really liked a piece of work, bar one stanza, or one comma, even! On these occasions, we've provided feedback to the writer in question to tell them our thoughts on the work, invite them to amend, and then invite them to re-submit. We would never want to interfere too much with someone else's writing, though, so the decision to go through this process always rests with the writer and what they're most comfortable with.

**Contact Details:**

dearreadersubmissions@gmail.com;

Twitter @dearreaderpoet;

Instagram: @dearreaderpoetry

*In Conversation with... Kellan Williams, Founding Editor*
*Worcester, UK*

**Pay? N Simultaneous submissions? Y Feedback? Y**
**Print Publication? N Online Publication? Y**

*We know that your main focus is poetry, but do you ever accept submissions which verge on cross-genre or which are stylistically different to the rest of your publishing aesthetic?*

Yes, absolutely.

*What is the editorial focus for your literary journal and what have you set out to achieve?*

The editorial focus of my journal is to create a space for under-represented voices in the Literary Community, and provide in depth feedback to those who benefit from it. As Founding Editor, I want to create a journal that excels in trends, is trusted by the community and provides a space for the minority of writers.

*When are your submission windows?*

Submissions are always open.

**Contact Details:**
theseafrontpress@outlook.com

# About the Editors

**Isabelle Kenyon** is a northern writer and the author of chapbooks: This is not a Spectacle, Digging Holes To Another Continent (Clare Songbirds Publishing House, New York, 2018), Potential (Ghost City Press, 2019), Growing Pains (Indigo Dreams Publishing Ltd, 2020) and one short story with Wild Pressed Books (Short Story 'The Town Talks', 2020). She is the Managing Director of Fly on the Wall Press, a socially conscious small press for politically-engaged poetry, fiction and anthologies. She has had poems and articles published internationally in journals such as Ink, Sweat and Tears and newspapers such as The Somerville Times and The Bookseller.

She was listed in the Streetcake Experimental Writing Prize 2020; 2019 and for The Word, Lichfield Cathedral Competition 2019. Her poems have been published in poetry anthologies by Indigo Dreams Publishing, Verve Poetry Press, and Hedgehog Poetry Press. She has performed at Cheltenham Poetry Festival and Verbose, Manchester in 2020, Leeds International Festival as part of the 'Sex Tapes', Apples and Snakes' 'Deranged Poetesses' in 2019 and Coventry Cathedral's Plum Line Festival in 2018.

She is currently working on her first novel: Dark Energy, which has been funded by Arts Council England. She is a fierce dog lover and a confessed caffeine addict.

**Dr Charley Barnes** is an academic and author from the West Midlands, UK. She is the author of several poetry publications, including: A Z-hearted Guide to Heartache (V. Press, 2018); Body Talk (Picaroon Poetry, 2019); Hierarchy of Needs: A Retelling, co-authored with Claire Walker (V. Press, 2020), and Lore: Flowers, Folklore, and Footnotes (Black Pear Press, 2021). Charley has also authored three short fiction releases: Death Is A Terrible House Guest (The Black Light Engine Room Press, 2019); Burn The Witch (The Black Light Engine Room Press, 2020) and Go On A Road Trip (Wild Press Books, 2020). Under Charlotte Barnes, Charley writes crime fiction, including the titles: Intention; The Copycat; The Watcher; and The Cutter (Bloodhound Books, 2019-2021). She has had individual poems and fiction pieces published by the likes of Ink, Sweat and Tears, Riggwelter Press, and Bind Collective.

Charley is the current Managing Director of Sabotage Reviews, the editor of Dear Reader, and a lecturer in Creative and Professional Writing at the University of Wolverhampton. She has spoken and performed at events such as Verve Poetry Festival, Cheltenham Poetry Festival, and Tamworth Literature Festival, where she formed part of a panel to discuss the practicalities of publishing crime for a contemporary readership. Charley was the Worcestershire Poet Laureate 2019-2020. She is now the Writer-in-Residence for The Swan Theatre, Worcester, and their associated venues. When she isn't writing, she's likely drinking tea, eating cake, or walking her dog.

# RESOURCES

**Places Isabelle Kenyon likes to go to for further submission opportunities...**

New Writing North newsletter
Writing East Midlands newsletter
Authors Publish (a newsletter and a website)
Angela Carr's monthly roundup: https://angelatcarr.wordpress.com/

**Places Dr. Charley Barnes likes to go to for further submission opportunities...**

National Associate of Writers in Education website
Writing West Midlands website
The Poets' Directory website

## About Fly on the Wall Press

A publisher with a conscience.
Publishing high quality stories, poetry and anthologies on pressing issues, from exceptional writers around the globe. Founded in 2018 by founding editor, Isabelle Kenyon.

## A sample of other publications:

*Bad Mommy / Stay Mommy* by Elisabeth Horan
*The Woman With An Owl Tattoo* by Anne Walsh Donnelly
*the sea refuses no river* by Bethany Rivers
*White Light White Peak* by Simon Corble
*Small Press Publishing: The Dos and Don'ts* by Isabelle Kenyon
*Grenade Genie* by Tom McColl
*House of Weeds* by Amy Kean and Jack Wallington
*No Home In This World* by Kevin Crowe
*The Goddess of Macau* by Graeme Hall
*The Prettyboys of Gangster Town* by Martin Grey
*The Sound of the Earth Singing to Herself* by Ricky Ray
*Inherent* by Lucia Orellana Damacela
*Medusa Retold* by Sarah Wallis
*Pigskin* by David Hartley
*We Are All Somebody*
*Someone Is Missing Me* by Tina Tamsho-Thomas
*Aftereffects* by Jiye Lee
*No One Has Any Intention of Building a Wall* by Ruth Brandt
*The House with Two Letter-Boxes* by Janet H Swinney
*The Guts of a Mackerel* by Clare Reddaway
*Snapshots of the Apocalypse* by Katy Wimhurst

## Social Media:
@fly_press (Twitter)
@flyonthewall_poetry (Instagram)
@flyonthewallpress (Facebook)
www.flyonthewallpress.co.uk